ADVENTURES OF ADAM AND ZARA IN ST. VINCENT AND THE GRENADINES
Copyright © 2022 by Sandrina Barrock-Lavia & Kinnike Mandeville-Leacock
Paperback ISBN: 979-8-9869100-6-2
Hardcover ISBN: 979-8-9869100-7-9
Library of Congress Control Number: 2022917902
Published in Austin, Texas USA

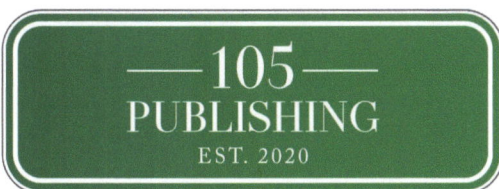

—105—
PUBLISHING
EST. 2020

"The more that you read, the more things you will know. The more that you learn, the more places you'll go."

- Dr. Seuss, I Can Read With My Eyes Shut!

To our dear Zara and Adam - Be kind. Be free. Be happy. Enjoy every adventure that life has to offer.

To Arin, Fari, Genesis, and Jehlanie - Be brave. Be awesome!

To Arya - Be as fearless as your dad!

Adventures of Adam and Zara in St. Vincent and the Grenadines

Written by:
Sandrina Barrock-Lavia
&
Kinnike Mandeville-Leacock

Illustrated by:

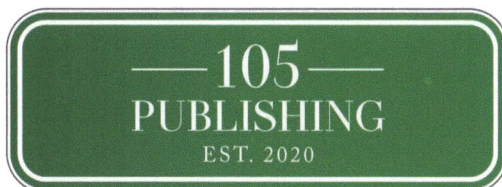

—105—
PUBLISHING
EST. 2020

Adam and his mom were at their home in Barbados, excited to take a trip to St. Vincent. Adam already had his suitcase packed, as he was ready to go!

"St. Vincent is an island in the Caribbean, with the inclusion of 32 cays, which are smaller islands called the Grenadines," Adam's mom explained. "Nine of these islands are inhabited - we will visit a few on the next trip. St. Vincent is the home of the oldest botanical gardens in the Western Hemisphere."

"Yes, mommy. I think we should visit the gardens first on this trip!"

St Vincent
&
The Grenadines

Excited about their trip, they scurried through the airport. When they arrived to the gate, Adam paused and then exclaimed, "No way, daddy. NO WAY! It's Zara!" Adam and Zara ran toward each other. Zara and her parents flew into Barbados so they could all fly to St. Vincent together.

"Surprise, Adam! You thought you were meeting us in St. Vincent, didn't you?" laughed Zara's mom.

"Oh, Auntie Sani and Uncle Andy, this is the best surprise ever, ever, ever!" Adam exclaimed as he and Zara walked off hugging each other, chatting endlessly.

"Hi Auntie K! Hi Uncle Fabian!" waved Zara.

Although Adam is three years younger than Zara, they had a very special bond from the first time they met. Every Tuesday and Saturday evening, Zara and Adam video-called each other where they played games on their tablets and spoke about their school friends.

They looked at the planes as they landed and patiently waited on their plane to St. Vincent.

"It's here," screamed the children as they gathered their things to get on the plane.

"Kids, did you know that Argyle International Airport was opened in 2017? It was built to replace the smaller airport which was called E.T. Joshua Airport," said Auntie Sani. "Some residents had to relocate, and now the area consists of schools, a plaza, and by-pass roads. Isn't that amazing?"

The children agreed as they listened intently.

Adam's grandparents picked up everyone from the airport. The children enjoyed the winding roads, going up and down the hill like a roller-coaster, fresh air, trees, animals, and landscapes as they drove to their homes.
The children were giggling as they swayed in their seats.

Adam and his parents stayed with his grandparents in a village called Fair Hall. Zara and her family stayed at their family home in a small town called Calliaqua.

Saint Vincent

Saint Vincent Passage

Fancy

▲La Soufriere Peak
3952 ft / 1205 m

Wallilabou

Chateaubelair

▲Richmond Peak
2207 ft / 673 m

Georgetown

Barrouallie

Colonarie

Colonarie

Layou   Vermont

Petite Bonhomme
▲ 1835 ft / 559 m

Biab

Mesopotam

Kingstown

Stub

Arnos Vale

Calliaqua

As promised, the parents took the children to the Botanical Gardens. Granny and Granddad came along to give the children a little history lesson on plants and animals. The children were fascinated with the tall trees, beautiful flowers, and colourful animals.

"Children, according to the history books, this is where the clone of a breadfruit tree was planted, which was brought into SVG by Captain Bligh in 1793. These trees have all been here for many years. They are older than you are," said Granddad.

"Wowwww," said the children in awe.

As they left the gardens, the children asked if they could try the breadfruit that granddad had roasted the day before.

"I'm happy that you want to try the breadfruit. Did you know that roasted breadfruit and fried jackfish is the national dish of St. Vincent and the Grenadines?" asked Granny.
"I'm allergic to fish, Granny," said Zara, "but I will try the breadfruit!"
Granddad and Uncle Fabian said they would take the children to the garden to pick fruits and vegetables only if they promised to relax for the rest of the day.

The next day, the children were up early for their next adventure. Can you guess where they were off to? They were off to the Leeward side of the island with more winding roads, as the children giggled uncontrollably. Their first stop was Fort Charlotte.

"Do you know what Fort Charlotte is?" Zara's dad asked the children. "It's a structure that was designed for the defense of the country from outside countries that might try to take over. Fort Charlotte was built by the British to protect the island from the Spanish. A long time ago, prisoners were also kept here. This area is where they baked bread."

"Look at the canons," said Adam's dad as he ran with the children to see the prison cells.

They went even higher to see the views.

They continued their journey on the winding road to the Leeward side of the island. The children were so amazed that they could see the houses below the road.

"That's called a valley. The village is called Barrouallie and it is known for its fishing," said Uncle Fabian.

"The village before was Layou. These are two smaller towns on the island. We will pass through another town as we continue," said Adam's mom.

As they drove further, they spotted something so magnificent that they both shouted "We see it! We see it!" Can you guess what they saw?

Yes, in all its beauty, the children spotted the peak of the volcano that they had heard so much about. "Did you know that it erupted several times in April 2021, Adam?" said Zara. Adam giggled. "Yes and we had ash all around our house and neighbourhood in Barbados. We had to stay inside with the windows closed for a few days. There was no school."

They drove to the furthest point on the island called Richmond. There they saw some of the heavy machinery used to remove the volcanic ash.

For the first time, the children were silent as they looked around at the burnt mountain top and at the river flowing into the sea with all the black stones around.

As they ate and drove back, Uncle Fabian decided to make one more stop before going home.
Can you guess where?

Yes, they arrived at Darkview Falls.

"Hold my hand, Zara. I crossed this before. You're safe with me!" Adam said as he led the way.

"We have a little climb to make before we get to the falls, okay?" he said as he followed Uncle Andy and guided Zara.

"Everything is so amazing. Wowww," said Zara.

Squeals and laughter could be heard echoing through the trees as they enjoyed their swim. They chatted all the way back to the car eating the locally made plantain chips and cassava chips. Can you guess where they're going next?

The beach! Yes, they stopped at Questelles Beach.

"Mommy, why is the sand black?" Zara asked before she and Adam stepped on it.

"Remember St. Vincent is a volcanic island, so the deposits are black. Barbados doesn't have a volcano, so its sand is almost white. Touch it. It feels the same."

The children tiptoed towards the sand.

The next day they went to the capital of the island.

"This is Kingstown," Uncle Andy explained. "The main town of St. Vincent. Many years ago, this area was the sea."

"Wow. Then what happened?" asked Zara.

"Well, there was a process called reclamation where the sea was pushed out and the area was filled to create new land."

"See that statue. It was moved there a few years ago when this big market was built. This is called Middle Street and runs from the top to the bottom of Kingstown, just like Back Street and Bay Street," explained Adam's mom. "There is a festival that happens in Kingstown nine days before Christmas every year called Nine Mornings, with local talents being showcased and bringing the Christmas feeling to the island."

After their tour, the children had some local food called Pelau, then headed to another beach.

"This beach looks like the ones in Barbados," Adam said.
Can you guess why?

Yes, because the sand was white. The children ran along the beach, built sandcastles, and had local soursop ice lollies to keep them cool in the beautiful sunshine while making plans for the following day.

Everyone packed their bags and got together for their final day of adventure. They drove along the wet road cautiously. The children observed that there were pockets of rain in different areas, but some places were dry and sunny. They had never seen that before.

"Wow, Daddy! Look at that," said Adam excitedly.

"This is called Rabacca Dry River because it is usually dry. Long ago, this bridge was not there so the people on the other side could not cross when the river was flowing heavily like this. The water came from the mountains that you see there and that is also the volcano, La Soufriere. Remember you saw it from the other side of the island a few days ago? Luckily, the bridge was built connecting both sides so the residents can go to school and work even when the river comes down," Adam's mom explained.

"Oh wow! Whoever came up with this bridge idea is brilliant!" Zara shouted.

"Let's cross it, daddy!" said Adam. Everyone walked across the bridge as Grandad drove across to meet them.

"Let's drive to the end of the island please," Adam suggested. They continued the narrow winding roads, passing Sion Hill, Point Village, Owia, then finally Fancy.

The little ones took lots of photos, ate more snacks, then started their journey back to Owia.

WELCOME
TO THE
CARIB COMMUNITY

Orange Hill

Over Land

Sandy Bay

Point

Owia

Fancy

Next, they went to Owia Salt Pond. "The water was so rough compared to the other beaches," Zara said. "Yes, because this is the Atlantic Ocean so it's quite rough. You can only bathe here when there is a low tide, but we wanted you to still see what it's like," said Auntie Sani.

They headed back to Rabacca Dry River where the rain had stopped, and the river was dry again. The children were fascinated that they got to see it go from wet to dry in such a short amount of time.
Can you guess where they were going?

Yes, to their final beach outing on this vacation.

"Salt Pond? Didn't we just come from here?"

"This is another Salt Pond. Can you tell the difference?"
As they approached the water, Zara said, "this is much calmer than the other."

"That's correct. It's because this beach is not as exposed to the Atlantic Ocean, so you can go in the water."
"Notice anything else?" Adam's dad asked.

"More sand than rocks!" Adam replied.
"Yep," chimed in Zara as she gathered her bucket to play on the sand with Adam.

"I don't want this vacation to ever end!" Zara commented as they built a sandcastle from the sand.

"Zara! I have a great idea!" said Adam "Why don't you visit me in Barbados for the summer? There are lots of places we can visit and exciting adventures we can go on. What do you think?"

BARBADOS

THE END!

ACTIVITY PAGE

LET'S TEST OUR MEMORY!

1)   Where did Adam meet Zara on the trip?

2)   Which island were they going to?

3)   What's the name of the airport on the island?

4)   What was the name of the first tourist site that they visited?

5)   What is the National Dish of St. Vincent and the Grenadines?

6)   Which side of St. Vincent is the volcano located?

7)   Why does St. Vincent have black sand?

8)   Where is St. Vincent and the Grenadines?

1)   _ O L _ A _ O

2)   B _ E _ D F _ _ I _

3)   _ A B _ C _ _ DRY _ I _ E _

4)   A _ G Y _ _ E I _ T _ R N A _ I _ N _ L A _ R P _ R _

5)   S _ N _ C _ S T _ E S

6)   _ E _ L A _ A _ T _ O _

7)   N _ N E M _ R N _ N G

8)   _ A _ K V _ _ W F _ L L _

A	G	B	R	I	O	X	T	E	E	R	T	S	H	O	L	N	W	N	Q
O	R	A	S	V	C	P	B	N	G	J	G	Q	B	L	U	L	N	A	K
E	R	C	R	O	E	N	I	H	S	N	U	S	S	W	H	S	H	E	H
N	I	J	G	D	N	L	C	V	A	D	G	O	C	G	S	H	J	B	K
O	W	I	A	H	E	O	V	H	J	K	H	D	F	G	I	F	D	B	S
I	B	N	M	L	P	N	O	H	I	B	G	A	D	F	F	A	S	I	S
T	Q	W	E	R	T	Y	S	O	U	I	N	B	I	O	K	P	A	R	S
A	D	F	T	E	K	R	A	M	S	M	F	R	G	H	C	J	K	A	H
C	Z	X	C	V	R	I	V	E	R	K	B	A	N	M	A	Q	W	C	E
A	E	R	T	R	Y	U	I	O	R	P	N	B	P	A	J	S	A	D	F
V	B	U	A	L	E	P	V	C	X	U	Z	L	R	L	K	E	J	H	G
N	K	J	K	L	Z	X	C	V	B	N	T	M	Q	I	B	W	E	R	T
T	N	E	C	N	I	V	T	S	Q	W	Z	N	X	C	D	V	B	N	M
Q	W	E	R	T	S	Y	U	I	O	P	L	J	E	K	H	G	F	D	S
A	Z	X	C	V	L	B	N	M	Q	P	O	I	U	V	Y	T	E	R	E
S	T	O	R	R	A	P	R	T	Y	M	K	A	U	I	D	O	P	F	S
F	R	E	W	Q	N	A	S	D	C	A	Y	S	F	G	H	A	J	K	L
I	S	L	A	N	D	G	F	D	S	P	A	H	W	E	R	T	C	U	I
S	H	J	K	L	M	N	B	V	C	X	Z	P	O	I	U	O	Y	T	R
H	X	Z	L	K	J	H	F	O	R	T	G	F	D	S	R	A	Q	W	E

HOME   BEACH   CAYS   MAP   BARBADOS   STVINCENT
ISLAND   CARIBBEAN   PARROTS   GARDENS   FISH
ROCKS   ASH   RIVER   VACATION   BRIDGE   ADVENTURE
SUNSHINE   OWIA   FORT   BRIDGE   PELAU   JACKFISH
MARKET   STREETS

About the Authors

Sandrina Barrock-Lavia was born in St. Vincent and the Grenadines. There, she was a certified family counsellor and she is now a registered educator in Toronto. Becoming a mother inspired her to pursue her passion for writing. While exploring the idea of writing her own book with her longtime friend Kinnike Mandeville-Leacock, they figured this was a great opportunity to embark on, as reading is fundamental and a great way for children to broaden their imagination. The inspiration for writing came after watching their children communicate during the pandemic and speaking about their family trips together. This idea became a reality and enabled them the opportunity to start their first series of children's books.

Kinnike Mandeville-Leacock is a Vincentian Architect and Project Manager. Kinnike fell in love with the subject of English literature while attending St. Vincent and the Grenadines Community College and promised herself that she would write a book someday. This dream of being an author materialized when Kinnike had her son Adam, and her longtime friend Sandrina Barrock-Lavia had her daughter, Zara. Both living away from St. Vincent, they embarked on this mission to showcase the Caribbean through the eyes of their children. The Children's books are written to teach them about their Vincentian heritage and to share the stories of their adventures, places of interest, and Vincentian culture with other children around the world. Ultimately, Kinnike and Sandrina wish to prove to Adam and Zara that dreams can become a reality and encourage them to dream and know that they can achieve whatever they put their minds to.

105 Publishing LLC
Austin, TX
www.105publishing.com

www.ingramcontent.com/pod-product-compliance
Lightning Source LLC
Chambersburg PA
CBHW042015080426
42735CB00002B/63